Can You See Us?

Twin Memoirs of a Teacher

TUCKER TWINS

Order this book online at www.trafford.com
or email orders@trafford.com

Most Trafford titles are also available at major online book retailers.

A Bles'd Production Inc. book, published by Trafford Publishing

Note for Librarians: A cataloguing record for this book is available from
Library and Archives Canada.

Printed in the United States of America.

ISBN: 978-1-4269-5848-9 (sc)
ISBN: 978-1-4269-5847-2 (hc)
ISBN: 978-1-4269-5842-7 (e)

Library of Congress Control Number: 2011902484

Trafford rev. 03/01/2011

www.trafford.com

North America & international
toll-free: 1 888 232 4444 (USA & Canada)
phone: 250 383 6864 ♦ fax: 812 355 4082

This book is a product of Bles'd Productions Inc.

It is dedicated to our children Jeremiah Bles'd Wicks, Adria Johnson, Adrian (AJ) Johnson. God children: Mekhi and Sade Wallace, Michaela Grace Newson, nephew Little Philip Tucker III, and all children everywhere. See the children. Here they are.

Hair: Black • **Eyes:** Dark Brown
D.O.B.: 4-25-94

Adrian Johnson

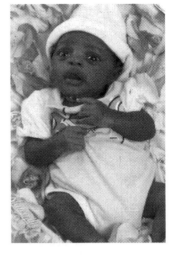

Adria Johnson

A special thank you to the staff of Bles'd Productions Inc. and my uncle Emeritus Dr. Willie George Tucker, our mother Mrs. Maretha Tucker, my father, Bishop Philip Tucker Sr., Brother, Rev. Dr. Philip Tucker Jr., and wife Dr. Pamela Jenkins-Tucker, sister Dr. Philetha Tucker-Johnson, Brother-n-law, husband, Coach Adrian Johnson and husband, Mr. Robert Wicks.

Disclaimer

Stories appearing in this book are created to ignite feelings for people to become involved in education. Any likeness to real people or real characters pertaining to the stories is purely coincidental. Names appearing in the book not including the dedication page or pertaining to the authors themselves are fictional.

Table of Contents

PREFACE

Drs. Phyllis and Philetha Tucker have been teaching most of their lives. Teaching became their passion. Throughout their careers, they have collaborated on projects, spoken at various educational venues, conducted educational workshops, formed a ministry team for children, and taught on the middle school, high school, and college levels. Born identical twins, they are similar in many ways.

The Tucker Twins attended the same schools growing up, went to the same piano lessons, and were in the same dance classes together. They broke racial barriers when schools became integrated and Dr. Philetha became the first junior, first female, and first African American student government president of their high school. Dr. Phyllis followed her lead and became the first African American senior class president. In that same year, both young ladies became the first African American head majorettes. They were very verbal about injustices, and withstood all obstacles placed before them in a time of racial inequalities. When Dr. Philetha decided to put on a school dance under her leadership as the first African American Student Government president, the principal called her into the office and told her she could not have the dance if she could not accomplish getting 350 tickets sold. Several Caucasian teachers called Caucasian students in their classrooms and told the students not to purchase the tickets. Two days before the dance, very few tickets had been sold. It was nowhere near the required number the principal presented. Dr. Phyllis explained the situation to their mother, and Mrs.

Tucker sprang into action. She purchased 350 tickets for the dance, and gave them to the students for free. This bold and commendable act was the biggest testimony to the Tucker Twins of how effective parental involvement in a child's education could be.

As time moved forward, the two young ladies decided to attend a historical African American college known today as Bethune-Cookman University located in Daytona Beach,Florida. While there, the young ladies wanted to continue being majorettes and were disappointed to find that there were no females dancing or twirling batons in front of the band.

The band was popularly known as The Marching Men Of Cookman. This did not stop their pursuit. The twins had conversations with the president of the college, and as a result, the Tucker Twins began to perform at pep rallies as the Golden Girls. Following their lead, other young ladies became vocal, and today, the well-known 14karat gold girls lead the Bethune-Cookman University band.

Dr. Philetha went on to become the first African American woman in the 63 year history of the pageant to become Miss Daytona Beach Florida. Dr. Phyllis and the Tucker family were never far behind in support. Once their college days were over, Dr. Philetha obtained her first teaching assignment in Hillsborough County Schools as an English teacher, while Dr. Phyllis completed her tour as Miss Black America.

This book will be written in one voice of two people who share the same educational views, and in some instances, the same or similar experiences.

Introduction

CAN YOU SEE US?
TWIN MEMOIRS OF A TEACHER

Imagine that you are a teacher. You come into school and prepare for your Homeroom class.

The Homeroom class is the class where all of the information is handed out to the children in your classroom that need to be taken home for parents to read and or sign. Make sure you collect all of the previous forms handed out the day before. Be sure to go over your classroom rules, stand for the pledge of allegiance, collect money for the lockers that have to be issued to students, and please don't forget to collect the lunch forms because the children must eat. Of course the students must watch the morning show announcements, and then there is Johnny, who just shot a rubber band at Sonia. Be sure to stop the altercation before writing a pass for Sashaseminey to go to the bathroom? Wait a minute. Rewind that? How do you pronounce Sashaseminey? Oh it's just as easy to pronounce as Bardaviaornsky, the other student's name you must remember how to say to make the students feel special.

Oh no. The bell is about to ring and there is an interruption over the intercom about students who need to have bus passes to ride the school bus in the afternoon. Those students must be sent to the office. However; they can't be sent to the office without a pass and you will need to write three of them for each student including Bardaviaornsky. His name alone will take at least two minutes to write (LOL). Oops, "LOL" is an acronym that you picked up while talking to a student who forgets to just laugh, so took a shortcut to say to you, "Dawg, you r funny, LOL."

In the meantime, a phone rings in the classroom. You must stop everything to find out whose phone it is. The policy written in the handbook is that cell phones are permissible in school but cannot be seen or turned on. If the phone is seen or turned on, the teacher will confiscate it and place it in an envelope. The teacher must then fill out paperwork, and is responsible for taking the cell phone to the office. The teacher must also call the parent and ask the parent to pick up the phone from the office.

Two students are now trying to attract your attention because they have to go to the bathroom. Nevertheless, you are still having trouble confiscating the cell phone from the student who has it because he is refusing to give it to you. You make it clear to the student that you will be calling his mother about his behavior, and he says to you," So what? She ain't comin heah. She don't come to nothing I do."

Just two minutes before the bell rings, you realize you have not called roll. You take out your roll book and tell the students to say "Here" if their name is called. You begin to struggle with some names while calling roll and never look up due to time. The bell rings and the students all rise to exit, and you never noticed the student who was up at your desk because he had something he needed to tell you. You never noticed Sherry wanting to tell you she was pregnant by a relative. You never noticed Maria needing to talk to you about a schedule change because English is her 2nd language. You never noticed Bobby, who needed to tell you about his feelings regarding his dad having to go to Iraq. You never noticed Raheem, who had been bullied for the past three days and needed your help. They were all at your desk while you were calling roll, confiscating cell phones, standing for the pledge, writing some passes or stopping someone from throwing a paper ball at another student. Before they exited your classroom, they were ALL in your face asking . . ." Can you see us?"

Chapter 1

My Children Need Your Help!

It was a sunny afternoon in August, 2010. I was sitting on my bed watching my favorite soap opera when someone kept knocking on the door. "Go away," I shouted. The knock became more and more violent. I was the only one at home at the time so I was forced to relinquish my comfort and go to the door. When I got closer to the door, I heard my 13 year old son crying for me to hurry and let him in. When he came in the door, he fell into my arms and began to cry. He was dirty and appeared to be very tired. His bus driver drops him off only two blocks away from the house so he doesn't have to walk too far coming home from school. Today was very different however.

As I helped him to the couch, he began to cry even louder. I immediately thought that he had gotten hurt at football practice as he kept rocking back and forth in my arms as I held him close to me. I kept asking what was wrong. Finally, he broke and told me that two teen boys at his middle school were charged with beating a 13 year old boy in the head with a baseball bat. The two boys ranging from 13-15 years old assaulted the classmate with a bat because he was openly gay. One of the teens had held the boy down behind the

1

school gym while the other assaulted him. Both teens were members of the math league team. The perpetrators were charged with false imprisonment and assault. The boy was continuously harassed by his two teammates for nearly two months before the assault. There was only one witness who came across the beating, and rather than do something, he ran.

A sickening, palpable feeling took over my stomach. "Jesse", I softly called his name. "Did you know the boys real well?" As Jesse looked up at me, he burst out into a more violent cry and said, "Mama, I was the one who ran." For a moment, I went into shock. The first thing that came to my mind was why hadn't the school notified me of what had happened in school that day? I ran to every room in the house to make sure my phones were operating and found that I had accidentally knocked one of them off the hook and I had missed five calls on my cell phone which was on vibrate. Just then, two police officers appeared at my door. It had started all over again.

In 2005, another son was off in college. He decided to pledge a fraternity. Johnny died during HELL WEEK. Junior fraternity brothers were told to be tough on the pledges. Johnny was ordered to the bathroom with two other pledges. Gerald, one of the pledges was ordered to release his feces in the toilet. Mark was ordered to wipe Gerald's butt. My Johnny was ordered to drink the toilet water and make himself throw up. All three were forced to urinate on each other and inhale the smell for an hour before being beaten by a paddle given ten licks on the bare rear.

All three were ordered to strip naked, they were blindfolded, and their hands were tied behind their backs. In the very cold weather around midnight, the three were driven to a cemetery and dropped off in three different locations. It was their job to get untied somehow, and find their way back to the frat house by morning. It was a long night for me and Johnny's dad. We were used to talking to our son every night. He had not called us and it became later and later. We tried calling some of the fraternity brothers but to no avail. The following morning the cops appeared at our door and told us they had found Johnny's naked cold body in a cemetery.

My baby had collapsed and had suffered a massive heart attack. Fraternity members didn't go back and check on any of the boys. Mark and Gerald both survived but ended up in serious condition in a hospital. Johnny's heart stopped at 5:00A.M. Needless to say, not one of the fraternity brothers was there. It had been hours before Johnny's father and I had learned how he died.

Hazing is illegal in the majority of states including California, At most, it is a misdemeanor, and the perpetrators usually get a slap on the wrist. Most colleges have banned hazing and some organizations have even been suspended, but that doesn't bring my boy back to me. A Hazing expert was quoted saying, "It's kinda like having unregulated gangs on campus, and yet it's a hidden problem that doesn't get discussed on the news a lot."

There is so much happening in schools and colleges that are not discussed in the news a lot. There are so many unknown policies and secrets that are hidden in a dark deep closet. Behind the closet door lies stories of all my children, my colleagues, my business associates within my profession, politicians, parents and all who are linked to education. They have been trapped for years screaming, crying, and holding on to each other waiting for help. Some grow old, and some grow too weak to reach the locked door. Some never make it out at all. Those who have made it out are those who still had the energy left who never grew tired or went to sleep when they saw an escape window open that was too small to bring friends along. Those who remain behind wait to see if those who have escaped will come back for them. Many are waiting for someone to just see them.

Two years earlier, my 12 year old daughter was a 7th grader in middle school. She was in the locker room when another female brought a gun in a bag. My daughter stated that Cindy, the girl with the gun in a bag, started talking to her and another girl when Cindy put the gun in my daughter's hand. My daughter immediately let Cindy know that she did not want to have anything to do with a gun and placed the gun back in the bag and went to gym class. I tried to convince the principal that some students do say no to criminal activity. It didn't matter.

According to the school officials, my daughter was guilty because she touched the gun and knew the gun was on campus and she didn't tell. The girl who originally had the gun and a few other students had gotten caught. The principal had gotten my daughter out of class and suspended her for ten days stating that the gun was in her hands and she knew the gun was on campus and didn't tell anyone. I asked my daughter why she didn't tell, and she told me that tattletales catch hell and snitches get stitches.

Thinking about "Snitches", I wish someone would have snitched on my 13 year old daughter who was given a prescription for emergency contraception by the school nurse at her school.

Since the school is under the "Title 1" status, the law is written that the students can be given birth control or an HIV test if the child is over 12. The only permission I had given the school was for them to give her an aspirin for a headache, and she ended up with birth control? What is wrong with this picture? The rage inside of me was about to boil over when I found out the school had taken control out of my hands as a parent.

Just inside 20 minutes of trying to cope with the information about my 13 year old daughter, I saw a news flash reported by ABC news on my youngest daughter's elementary school giving out condoms without parental permission. Since when is it ok for a school to provide tools for sexual pleasure? As I was about to deal with this issue, I was being called by a co-worker who was screaming in the background, "They've been shot! They've been shot!" "Who's been shot?," I screamed. Later I found out that two of my children had called in a bomb threat at their high school and did a drive-by shooting when the school was evacuated. The lives of teachers and students were gone in a split second on that very sad day.

I didn't have much time to grieve because one of my colleagues had shown up at my home to let me know that she was going to jail for having just fought my 10th grade daughter in the classroom, as my other daughter took out her cell phone and caught it all on camera.

It didn't stop there. My husband quickly ran into the room to tell me that our other high school son was so stressed out over pressure to excel in school, he set fire in the bathroom trash can at his prestigious private school. He's only 17. I was relieved that charges were not filed, but rather, he was ordered to see a psychologist.

I have been in this business for over 20 years and I have seen it all. There have been 5 killings, rape, murder, assault with a deadly weapon, bomb threats, homicide, and other heinous acts in this business. I know you must be thinking that I either wear a badge or work somewhere in a Law Enforcement office. Well, you're wrong. I'm a school teacher. I have 28 years of stories inside of me to tell!

Chapter 2

From My Beginning

I started teaching in 1984. Boy, have things changed. When I was coming through school, I only had to worry about tardies, fights, and maybe a little profanity. Our student handbook did not look like the student handbooks today. Have you even read one lately? On the inside cover it tells you what won't be tolerated in the school. There are over 24 CRIMES listed.

Additionally, the book lists where students may go for help if needed. I tell the children every year, their student handbook should be their Bible in school. It may be the only protection they have. There are so many resources in the handbook that can guide a student to safety precautions, and ultimately, safety. However, if they don't read it, and many of them don't, they sometimes set themselves up to be victimized, stepped on or set-up. There are millions of children who are bullied each year. Then we read headlines like this: Catholic School Vandalized . . . Nine Year old Suspended For Hate Crime . . . . . . Boy raped By Hockey Stick And Broom Stick.

I am outraged when I read headlines like this. My 8 year old biological son is my only child. I could not imagine my only son coming to me with stories like these. Unfortunately, there are countless stories like these happening in schools across America. The news is inundated with criminal activity going on in schools. What is wrong with this picture? Well, let's look at it very hard. Close the book for a minute. Don't forget where you left off because I am going to share some stories with you that may shock you. Well maybe not shock, because after 29 years and seeing it all, nothing shocks me anymore.

I did not always have a passion for teaching. My passion grew as I grew. I grew more mature in my profession and I had to grow up fast. My mother had always said that education was impractical. It took me years to figure out what she was talking about. Now I know. I had come out of college very blue. I thought teaching would be so easy. After all, all I had to do was go into my classroom, set some rules, and teach. Wrong answer.

I remember one of my earlier teaching experiences. I had a classroom full of boys. I was working in an inner city school where parents were not as involved with their children as I had seen in schools located in the elite neighborhoods. Students were a little more playful then.

It's just that I didn't know how playful until I had my first encounter with Rashawn Baker.

Rashawn was quite a delightful young man, but he sought out laughter from his fellow classmates. He was always looking for a laugh. I was not prepared to handle the class clown.

Class clowns 101 was not taught in our college classes as we prepared for "teacherhood". I remember when Rashawn would enter class and sit in the very back. He would pick up a book and put it between his legs and begin to hunch. I probably would not have noticed if it had not been for Leroy shouting loudly, "Ms. Tucker, Rashwan is hunching a book!" The entire class turned their attention to Rashwan and that

8

was all he needed. The class burst into laughter and I couldn't help but laugh too. This was 8th grade.

After hunching the book for about a minute or two, I, along with the class, regained my composure and proceeded to teach a lesson on the board. It took a while for me to turn around and face the class as I had so much information to write. When I finally turned around, all 20 boys had on dark shades and started laughing. It was apparent that they were not paying any attention to anything I was saying. I asked Josh to summarize what I had just said. Josh had a slick grin on his face and nonchalantly mummered, "Umunh. "I don't know. I'm just admiring the view." "We all are," shouted Rashawn. The class burst into laughter.

At the time, I was wearing a dress and began to feel self conscious. Again, Rashawn began to hunch. This time he was using notebook paper. I was then compelled to write a referral and sent him to the office. When I asked him to come up to my desk and take his referral to the office, he "pimped walk" to the desk drawing more laughter from the class, and dove on my desk wagging his tongue like a dog. It took a while to regain control of the class, but it didn't last long when Rashawn returned to class with a paper bag. "I thought I told you to go to the principal's office with your referral," I said. "I did", he responded. "Well, why are you back?" "Because the principal started laughing at the referral and sent me to the nurse. That's why I have this bag. The nurse said my hormones were in full gear and I needed some pamphlets to read." The class roared with laughter. That's when it hit me. Mom said education is impractical. No one told me about the Rashawn Bakers I would have in class.

For as long as I remember, many students have had issues. Another student I remember was Macy. I had no idea that Macy admired me so much. I think a little too much. We had answering machines back in that time period. I was living with my mother at the time.

I happened to check the answering machine one day and heard a voice message from Macy directed to me. The voice was soft and appeared to be sensuous in the sense that someone was trying hard to sound sexy. The message went as follows: "Hi Miss Tucker. Dis Macy. I just want you to know that I love you. I want to lick you and kiss you all over. Let me know if you want to lick me and kiss me too." Then there was a short and faint giggle. I was shocked. I played the message back for my mother as I was looking for my roll book to find Macy's mother's phone number. None of my college professors had ever addressed an 8th grade student liking the teacher when I was in college. The only thing I knew to do was to address this situation with Macy's parents. When I reached Macy's mother, I told Mom what her daughter had done and her mother began to refute the allegations. "My daughter would never do anything like that," she said. She got angry with me for calling her about the matter, and I told her the message was captured on my answering machine. Macy's mother demanded that I play the message for her and I did. Needless to say, her mother apologized profusely and began shouting and cursing at her daughter while I was on the phone. The next day, I made arrangements to have Macy removed from my classroom.

As time moved forward, selling drugs in the neighborhood became more and more popular among the students. I remember Carl, who had failed twice and was still in 8th grade. Carl was a very well-dressed young man who used to wear so many gold chains around his neck that he could never walk upright because the chains weighed so much. He had what is considered the "pimp walk" as well. This was the cool walk. It was the walk that said I'm cool. Carl would keep wads and wads of money in his pocket.

I remember one day he came up to me and asked if he could buy me a pair of shoes. I tried to explain to Carl that selling drugs was going to get him a quick way to his grave. When I had asked the students in his class what they wanted to grow up and be, Carl showed no hesitation when he stated a drug dealer. I told him at that time that he would not live to be 21. Several years later, a co-worker brought me the morning paper and I read the headlines: STUDENT SHOT IN THE HEAD AFTER DRUG DEAL GOES BAD. Carl was dead at 19.

All of these stories took place in junior high school when we had football games and real basketball games. We had 7th, 8th, and 9th grade, where fun was on the tip of many tongues.

Teachers didn't hesitate to go to students' homes to talk to parents, and corporal punishment was embraced. However, there were still the issues.

I recall when I was teaching 9th grade and Randy was the only student I had who was driving to school. He too had failed and was 16. He was also married to a student at a local high school in the area. What made Randy unique was that he was the nephew of a well know drug Lord in the area. Randy didn't hesitate to talk to me about some of the activities of his closest uncle. I didn't know whether to believe him or not. I remember when he told me about a man who made his uncle mad and his uncle had the man's thumb cut off and sent to the man's family. I thought at the time that children certainly have good imaginations. It wasn't until a good period of time that I noticed Randy had missed 2 ½ weeks of school. When he returned, I asked him where had he been. That's when he told me that he had shot a man on a certain street due to a road rage situation. He then drove his car to his uncle's house and his uncle switched his car tag out and put Randy on a boat out of here. Once everything was cleaned up, Randy was able to come back to school. I again thought that children really do have great imaginations. Randy knew I did not believe him so he brought me a newspaper with every detail there was about the story. There was a key detail that no one could know but him that made me a believer. I told Randy not to tell me any more of his "mafia" stories. The last time I saw Randy was at the mall. His uncle had since died. Randy had a new wife and he had bought a huge home. He invited me over and his home took my breath away. Randy couldn't have been any more than 25 at that time.

Time was steadily moving forward. I have seen the FBI arrest a student who had written an essay on how to build a bomb. This was not the time to write about building bombs due to the Oklahoma bombing had just happened. Bomb threats and any mention of bombs was taken seriously by administrators in the schools. So when Jelecia, an 8th grader, got mad at one of her classmates and said she was going to blow the school up with a twinkie, she was suspended for three days. People were now becoming more and more fearful.

Things were getting crazy. It wasn't just students, it was everybody. During that time period, when teachers were being evaluated, they had the carbon copy evaluation forms. I distinctly remember standing outside the office of an Assistant principal. The AP had just gone over an evaluation with a teacher and told her to sign her name. The AP gave the teacher the carbon copy of her evaluation, and when the teacher left the office, the AP told me she didn't like the teacher so she started adding negative information that was filed in the principal's office.

I'll never forget having a conversation with one of the football players. He said, "Teach, you just don't know Coach Brown. When he shows us the films of the games, all we are watching is what is between the legs of the cheerleaders. Coach has instructed the cameraman to do close—ups of the cheerleaders' "coochies". We see splits, tumbles, cartwheels, and lifts. But the main focus is the "coochie". I then asked him why none of the players reported the coach. The player's response was, "Because teach, coach tells us, when we do something wrong, he won't see us. If he does something wrong, he doesn't want us to see him.

Chapter 3

WHO THE HELL IS THE EXPERT?

As time was moving, children were changing. Bigger issues were becoming a part of their lives. Government was not the same. Parents seemed to become more scarce in schools. But there were certain things that I noticed that did not change, and more than likely will never change. From then to now, the Pledge Of Allegiance has not changed. "Right and Wrong" has not changed. "In God We Trust" on the money has not changed. The basics of reading writing and arithmetic has not change. Bad and good has not changed. The foundation of religion has not changed. Everyone will always have a mother and a father. The basic needs of people: food clothing and shelter has not changed, and the only book written that has lasted for over 2000 years is the Bible. You may wonder why I am writing this. Well, here it is.

In my earlier years of teaching, I was recognized as a teacher. I decorated my classroom each year. I developed lessons that were in the best interest of my students. I called and kept in touch with parents to make sure they were on the same page with me and their child. I developed rules that students had to follow in my class. I hugged a child when he cried. I gave out my telephone number when a child needed to talk to someone when no one was at home. I took a child home when a parent forgot to pick him or her up after staying for a club after school. I took professional development workshops. I read books, and I went back to school to obtain another degree. I was not held soley accountable for the child's education. If a child was suspended, a letter was sent home by the student and the student could not return to school without the parent coming in for a conference. Parents were held responsible too. As a teacher, I educated the "whole" child. We played games and I learned who my students were. I worked with the product given to me. Many of my students were successful and some were not.

Nevertheless, I taught children. I did not teach tests.

School is no longer the way I knew it. Things look different now. The teacher seems to be fading away from the picture. I can no longer decorate my room as I'd like. I am being told now how to decorate my class. "You must have a word wall. You must have a curriculum wall. You must have student work wall. You must have an accolade wall. You must have an objective wall", the administrators say. "Let's make sure all of us have the same rules in our class", says the team leader. Supplementary material? Is it doable when you're on a timeline to finish a lesson for evaluation? Teachers are now being told when to teach the material, how to teach it, and given deadline dates to complete the lessons. It is hard to hug a child now for fear that another child will capture it on camera and post over the internet. When you contact the parent now, you may meet resistance or you may not reach them at all. If a child is suspended today, he or she is just suspended. No one is asking the parent to come to school so the child may come back anymore. After all, the teacher is the one being held soley accountable for the child now. The village is fading as well. Where are the churches? Oh that's right. Someone came up with a bright idea to take prayer out of schools, so that was the beginning to losing the connection to one of our three major institutions. And the home? Well, let's just say that now when we ask the student for a home phone number, the student's response may be, "Which home, my mother or my father's? The traditional two parent home is gone. The only institution left is school. This is the home where students spend at least eight hours a day, five times a week, and sometimes even longer if they participate in sports. I only wish I had more control over my home, which is my classroom.

In 1998, I remember when teachers were told that they were going to have to be trained in giving a state writing test to students. I studied the test for its first three years of inception and learned the format. I had learned the format so well, I started coming up with various activities to match students' learning styles. Later, a name would be given to this method called "Differentiated Instruction". In an effort to generate more student involvement, I had students in one of my classes to review the entire writing program put before us and had them to generate questions that might arise about the topic before whole group discussion. In that class, students had to pre-read the district's writing packet in order to identify the concepts they didn't understand, and to generate one or two questions concerning the concept.

Students then had to meet in pairs and talk about their questions. After the paired discussions, I listed the questions on the board. Students read carefully and purposefully as they searched for answers to their questions. This all happened before I had explained the concepts. The students were more engaged with this concept. After all was said and done, the pre-reading group out performed all the other classes. More discussions took place in all classes to determine why.

This was later called, CRISS strategy, later known as AVID strategy, later known as Kagan strategy, when in actuality it was just a teaching strategy. Why do we continue to put new names on old stuff? It is so frustrating for a teacher to attend professional workshops to find that he or she is already using the strategy that is being shown by the workshop presenter. For so long, teachers have continued to buy-into old sayings. It is now time to step back and take a look at the whole picture. For example, when Jr. High School was dissolved and replaced by middle schools, administrators preached "Flexibility." They told us we must be flexible. The following year, it was consistency. We must be consistent. The year after that it was diversity.

We must all respect diversity. I ask the question. What do these words have in common? You cannot be flexible and then be consistent while respecting diversity. It makes no sense.

Educators then say, "All children can learn." If all children can learn, then why are tens of thousands of them failing the state test? I hear some educators say, "The 'true' parent believes in Corporal punishment. However, once word is out that a parent spanked his child for bad behavior in our class, then we want to call 1-800 abuse hotline. Even some experts will tell you that there is a category for exemplary teachers, but there is always room for improvement.

Huh? If there is always room for improvement, then how can you reach exemplary status? That would seem unattainable. The hypocrisy in that statement to me is baffling. This is why we have the "highest score" possible. This is why there is an outstanding or a Doctorate or an expert! To give the statement any meaning, it would be best to say, "If you have not reached Exemplary, then there is room for improvement. Once you have reached exemplary, you should be creating "Wowsers" in your career. You are now so good at what you do that you are creating wowsers all the time. This is what mastery is all about. This is how you get to be the expert!

Each year, states and districts will meet to talk about what is happening in my house. They have no clue of what is going on in my house because nine times out of ten, they have never been to visit. After they put a packet together on how MY house should be conducted, they then present the packets to my principal, and the principal will tell me how I WILL conduct my house. If I do not comply to the rules set forth by the state and the district, then my evaluation will determine if I am going to be evicted out the home that I built and assisted in nurturing doctors, lawyers, entertainers, teachers, and the like for the past few years. Is the packet presented worthy of my attention? Maybe, maybe not. The point is, I have been doing my job for countless years. Each year I have gotten better and better. I have learned new things from others and began to create my own.

As I saw students change, I had to change, but the basics still remained the same. I have gotten so good at what I do I have now become a master at my career. My track record speaks for itself as I have raised test scores, tutored teachers and students, written a couple of books, and constantly read research as I am a Dissertation advisor for many principals, teachers, and supervisors working on their Doctorate degrees. I currently teach at two colleges and two major universities, and I have been teaching in middle school for over 29 years. In my growth, teaching has become a passion. The passion has turned into mastery.

Dave Ellis (2009) describes the master student as one who has attained a level of skill that goes beyond technique. For a master, methods and procedures are automatic responses to the needs of the task. Work is effortless; struggle evaporates. The master carpenter is so familiar with her tools they become a part of her. To a master chef, utensils are old friends. Because these masters don't have to think about the details of the process, they bring more of themselves to work. Mastery can lead to flashy results. For example, in basketball, an unbelievable shot at the buzzer.

I remember when I interviewed with the principal at my current school. She said to me, "I currently have 84% of my students passing. What can you do?" I looked at her, smiled, and told her I could move 98-99%, and by the end of the school year, I did!

The term 'expert' as described by the free online dictionary is a person with a high degree of skill in or knowledge of a certain subject. The highest grade that can be achieved in marksmanship. Of course P.J. Plauger, *Computer Language*, March 1983 states, "My definition of an expert in any field is a person who knows enough about what's really going on to be scared." Think about that for a moment. Things can get pretty scary when you feel like you're fading away. As an expert in my field, I believe the TRUE expert is one who gathers information from other known experts in his or her field. The TRUE expert will then create lessons using various ideas that will be in the best interest of what or whomever he or she is preparing for. For example, if I prepare a meal for my children, I must make sure I have the right ingredients for them to want to consume the meal. Since all of my children are different, I will need to use a little bit of this, and a little bit of that to fix the best plate for everyone! If you have made a down payment on your home over 20 years ago by going to college and obtaining a degree, and through the years, you made upgrades through professional developments and obtaining more degrees, and you are now creating "wowsers" in your career, YOU then are the expert!

Suppose one day you hear this. BREAKING NEWS . . . A tornado has just been spotted heading towards your house. It has done major damage in some areas, and some of your house has been hit. You've lost some of your children. However, some have sought out shelter in the closet. The Expert would have prepared for this moment by obtaining homeowners insurance a long time ago to keep his house standing. I wrote my own policy several years ago known as

PASSION. This is the best homeowners policy you could have. P= Parents. Call them.

Bring them back! A= Attitude. Have a great attitude towards children! S= Safety. Make students feel safe! S= Stakeholders. Bring the village back! I= Know that "I" am the expert in my house.

Take it back! O=Own your home. If the Landlord can't fix the problem with the materials they bring you, use your own! N= Now. The time is now! If you do not consider yourself the expert of your house after 15 years, then perhaps you should sell it to someone else. That is the key to being able to actually see your children.

Chapter 4

ASSESSING THE DAMAGE/TEACHER STORIES

The Naked Truth

Special Education Teacher . . . "I had a student in my class who was labeled EBD. EBD stands for Emotional Behavior Disturbed. Under this umbrella, a Special Education teacher may have many students who have conditions that need special attention. In this case, Joseph was very special. When Joseph would get upset, he'd want to fight. He would begin to rip off all of his clothes in front of the class. The interesting thing about Joseph was that he did not wear any underwear. I would have to call the office and an assistant would have to bring clothes kept in the office to my classroom. Since Joseph was a little large, the clothes did not fit him well and he found himself wearing what is known to the kids as "Hoochie" shorts. "Hoochie" shorts are those tight skin fitting shorts where you could almost see through the crotch area. Joseph would then tie the shirt in a knot and show his stomach. Whenever I called his mother to bring him extra clothes, she would never show up. Unfortunately, when Joseph got tired of wearing the too tight clothing, he would rip those clothes off. When his mother would pick him up after school, he would be draped in sheets as he had no clothes and his mother refused to send Joseph with an extra pair each day."

Don't Cut The Fool

ESOL Specialist . . . Marcus was labeled EBD and ESOL. ESOL means English as a second language.

When Marcus entered the school in 6th grade, he was initially misplaced as he should have been a fulltime student in the Special Education classes. Marcus had been raped by his mother and father when he was younger. Both parents have since passed away. Marcus is currently living with his grandmother. When Marcus was placed in the Regular Education class, he could not sit down, and he was always picking up items. Once, Marcus had a pair of scissors in his hand. He continued acting as though he was going to cut people in the class. The teacher in the class had instructed Marcus to put the scissors down several times. Marcus did not wish to comply. Finally, Marcus waved the scissors at the teacher and put the scissors up to his own throat as though he was threatening the teacher with the scissors by indicating he would cut the throat of the teacher.

At point Blank Range

High School Teacher . . . It was a normal day in class. I had told the students to take out a pencil and some paper because I was going to give them a test. I realized that during my break, I had left my answer key across the hall in my colleague's classroom, so I told the students to take out their notes to study. I would only be a minute. I went across the hall. I must have been there no more than three minutes when I heard a loud noise coming from my classroom. I knew this wasn't good because children had dashed out of the classroom screaming. When the other teacher and I ran over to the class, with her entire class as well, there lay in a pool of blood, Manuel, who had shot himself in the head at point blank range in the classroom. I froze for a moment while my colleague was screaming for the other students to evacuate the building. I then threw up all over myself. The only other thing I remember was Sharon, another student who was in the class at the time of the shooting, taking off her shirt to make a guaze to press against the bullet wound. I retired that year.

Drop Dead Gorgeous

High School Student

She was a drop dead gorgeous senior . No. I mean it for real. You can't have sex with her though. While in school she had full blown aids. This is the new way to communicate to your friends in high school. If anyone has a cell phone, facebook, or my space, beware if you are known to be a "skank or hoe". Once your business is put out there, you are labeled for life. Boys who had slept with Rosie had sent her picture via cell phone text messaging that she had given them aids. Everyone will always remember her as the one who killed so and so. That is what happened to Rosie before she left high school. She had slept with over 62 guys at the school, before rumor had it that the reason she left school was because she had aids. Later, her picture appeared in the obituary. Rosie died. Now over 62 boys were affected with the deadly disease.

Who Am I?

High School Student

I remember it well. I still laugh about it. Jerry was sitting in class putting on lipstick he had taken from his purse. I was sitting right next to him as he carefully put on other makeup. Everyone in the class knew he was gay. While the teacher was giving her lecture, Jerry appeared to become more and more agitated as he tried to get the details of his lips perfect via the lipstick. In the middle of the teacher's lecture, Jerry twisted up to the front of the classroom with his purse as he drew so much laughter from his classmates including me. "Ms. Irns, May I go to the bathroom?" You could tell the frustration of Ms. Irns as she had to stop her lecture to address Jerry's question. She told Jerry several times to sit down as she called his name loudly each time. Jerry stated to her that his name was not Jerry, and he wished to be called Sherry. The class laughed even harder. When the teacher told Jerry she would not address him by using the name Sherry, Jerry walked out of the classroom as the teacher warned she would be calling his mother. Once Jerry was out of the door, I remember Ms. Irns picking up her phone and calling Jerry's mother. It was very quiet in the class as Ms. Irns had her phone on speaker mode. Jerry's mother had told Ms. Irns she would be to the school in five minutes. When Jerry returned to class, he twisted to his seat and continued to put on makeup. Ms. Irns carried on as if nothing had happened. After about five minutes, I noticed someone peering in the window as if he or she was looking for someone. As I glanced a little harder, I recognized the woman at the door peeking in was Jerry's mother. When his mother's eyes became fixed on him, she burst into the classroom with a shoe. Literally all of Jerry's makeup flew in the air as his mother entered the classroom outraged and shouted, "Jerry Eucaliptis Bowman, what the hell are you doin?" She beat him all the way out the classroom with her shoe. We found out later that Jerry's mother had no clue her son was gay, and the shock of it all made her very ill. We never saw her again at school. That was a funny moment for me.

Will You Be My Mama?

Middle School student story

Cynthia was a shy quiet student. She never raised her hand in class to answer any questions. One day, being the teacher that I am, I asked her if anything was bothering her. Her response to me was, "Will you be my mama?" At first I was a little baffled. Then she told her story. "My mother, sister, and grandmother were in the truck behind us," she said. The family was headed to a wedding. Cynthia was riding in the car with her father as her mother, grandmother, sister and brother were in the truck behind them. Cynthia had glanced in the rearview mirror and saw her mother's truck flipping over off the interstate and began screaming for her father to turn around. When her father was able to return safely to the accident, Cynthia and her dad had jumped out of the car as others had stooped to help. Rescue personnel were called and on the way. In the meantime, Cynthia's sister had flown out of the car and was dead on impact. Her mother had a gash in her head and was semi conscious but bleeding badly. Her grandmother's legs were crushed as the truck had landed on them. "Mama died," she said. "They all did. Will you be my mama?"

"Yo Mama Looks Like King Kong!"

Middle School Teacher

It was a great day for the most part. However, Leroy was really getting on my nerves that day. I Kept telling him to be quiet while I handed graded papers back to the students. When I handed Leroy his paper back with an "F" on it, he got really upset. He started yelling at me and calling me names. I warned him several times to close his mouth. Finally Leroy told me he was going to get his mother on me. I looked at him and said, "Son, if your mama doesn't look like King Kong, then it is perfectly fine. Bring her in." Back in the day, parents didn't have to have clearance to walk on school grounds. The next day, this great big old thing came to my classroom dressed just like a sheriff. It was His mama." She said, "I heard you said I look like King Kong." Needless to say, things worked out ok when I told Leroy's mother how the conversation really went in class the day before. She became very upset with Leroy. She explained to me that

I was not the only teacher that Leroy had threatened her with. She and I worked out a plan to assist Leroy, and sadly, years later, when Leroy came back to thank me for being a good teacher, his mother had passed away.

I Don't Like White People

Elementary School Teacher

I remember when seven year old Dee-Dee came to school everyday and started as many fights as she could with white people. If you were white, she would skip you in the lunch line and start a fight. She would elbow you or kick you. One day, I pulled Dee-Dee aside and had a long talk with her. "What is your problem?" I asked. Finally, she told me that she hated white people. You see Dee-Dee lived in the projects. All she saw was violence in her neighborhood. She told me that the white policeman shot a black boy in the back and she saw it while he was running out the neighborhood store with some bags of candy. "They didn't have to shoot him," she said. "I hate white people!." Then she spat on a white student and got suspended.

How Did I End Up In Court? I'm A Teacher! (Part1)

Middle School Teacher

When he first entered my classroom he sat in the back of the class. He was quiet and well behaved. When he addressed me, he would say, "Yes ma'am. No ma'am." I thought he was the most adorable kid around. The students all called him Peno. They seemed to know him quite well.

One night while watching television, I saw a replay of a police car chase that had happened earlier that afternoon. Three teens had committed an armed robbery at a popular club. In the parking lot, two unmarked police cars were in the parking lot of the club, and the officers seemed to have been watching for criminal activity. Two of the teens robbed patrons in the parking lot at gun point, while the other was in the driver's seat of the stolen vehicle waiting. The chase started and ended up in a field where all three teens had jumped out of the stolen vehicle, and police pursued with dogs. One of the children was bitten on the leg by the dog. It was Peno. I was literally shocked. It was the talk at the school the next day. Students were all saying how Peno would not learn. I questioned what they meant by the statement. One student asked, "Don't you know? Peno has a long criminal record." I could not believe my ears. I refused to believe that this very respectful child who was so quiet in my class, and never had anything but the upmost respect for me, had a criminal record. Nonsense I thought. It wasn't until I received a phone call from his dad asking me if I would go to court and speak for his son about his character.

For me, this was a lot to ask since I have always taught my students to think before they act, and to remember that they would have to pay for their poor decisions. Dad had explained to me that Peno was more of a follower and that he was an innocent child who got caught up following friends. He begged me to go to the jailhouse to talk to Peno because he thought I was the only teacher that could have an impact on him. I did not know that Peno had thought so highly of me as he spoke a lot about me at home. After much nudging, I decided to go to visit Peno in jail.

The Jailhouse Visit (part II)

I went to jail, and I can assure you it was to visit my student and nothing else! Later on in the book you will see why I needed to clarify this. I spoke to Peno. It was very disheartening for me to see him. He seemed so remorseful and began to cry as he told me of the events that unfolded that day. "I was at work. My friends kept telling me that they wanted to pick me up from work and that we would ride around. Mark's mother had let him hold her car, and he told me I could drive it when they came and got me. When I went to the car after work, Mark gave me the keys and told me to drive to the club. I had no idea that they were about to rob anybody, and I certainly didn't know that the car was stolen. Please Ms. Tucker. Please come to court and speak for me," he said. As the tears rolled down his cheeks, I wiped them away and told him to make me a promise. I made him promise me that he would get his life together and come to church with me on Sundays. He agreed.

The next week, word got out that I would be going to court to speak on Peno's behalf. Students tried so hard to discourage me. They told me I had no idea what I was doing. They continued to tell me that Peno had a lengthy record, and that it would be a bad move on my part. I became a little more hesitant after some of my colleagues started telling me the same thing in the faculty lounge. "The kid is worthless," one teacher said. "He is rude and disrespectful. He deserves every bit of punishment he gets," said another teacher. "Is there anyone, who is willing to go to court with me and speak on this child's behalf?" I asked. Only one other teacher spoke up and agreed to go with me.

Prior to going to court, I had lengthy talks with Peno, and even got my father involved who is a Bishop at our church. He and I would visit Peno and pray with him. I told Peno I wanted him to come to church if the judge had mercy on him to let him out. Peno made many promises to go straight.

I Went To Court (Part 111)

I will never forget that morning. I showed up in the courtroom. I saw Peno's father, who gave me a most comforting nod of approval. All of a sudden, Peno's mother came into the courtroom and started shouting at Peno's father. They were both removed from the room and they took their argument outside. Just then, the Baliff had asked for all spectators in the courtroom to rise for the Honorable Judge. Prisoners were ushered in through a side door and my eyes looked into Peno's eyes of embarassment as he was shackled from his hands to his feet. The judge called case after case, and then he finally called Peno.

When Peno approached the bench, the judge got up, walked over to the side of the bench, and picked up what appeared to be a huge stack of papers from a table. The stack appeared so heavy that the judge herself, seemed to have had a problem lifting it and she dumped it on the table in front of her. She leaned over and immediately shouted at the attorney who was defending Peno. "Peyland, she said, How dare you come into my courtroom and make a mockery out of it defending this man. He has been in and out of jail, and boot camp, and we have given him every chance in the world to straighten up his act." She turned her attention to Peno and asked, "What do you have to say for yourself young man?" Peno seemed as though he was going to blame the split up of his mother, and his unstable life growing up until the judge told him to be quiet. She stated to him not to use what has happened in his life as an excuse to hurt others. The judge also made a surprising move. She asked that the families who were robbed that day be ushered into the courtroom. I had to look into the eyes of a crying mother, daughter, and an angry father. The judge heard from the family who wanted the maximum sentence for Peno. Peno was then asked to address the family. In a very remorseful tone. Peno apologized to the families and the judge adjourned for recess.

The Verdict (part1V)

When the judge re-entered the courtroom, she seemed very frustrated. She asked that Peno's teachers step forward. I spoke on behalf of Peno and told the judge that I would take full responsibility for Peno if she would have a little mercy. I told her that I would see to it that he attends church, and I would work with him. The judge paused a few minutes and spoke. "After hearing from the victims and hearing from the teachers, I'm sure you are not going to like what I am about to do," she said while looking at the victims. She then turned her attention to Peno and said, "Son, I am sentencing you to 5-10 years on each account, but I am suspending your sentence and sending you to a halfway house. If I ever see your face in my courtroom again for any reason, you will go to prison for life Is that clear?"

I monitored Peno for quite some time. I went to visit him every other day, accepted collect calls from him, and often took my father with me to pray for him. I would pick Peno up for church on Sundays, and he really began to change his life. Once he had finished his time, he disappeared. It would be years later when I saw him again. He was a manager in one of the local restaurants, had married and had five children. It was a moment in time I would never forget, and that was the ONLY time I went to jail.

Whew! What a lot of damage the storm has caused. There is so much to clean up. The three major institutions seem out of reach. The home is gone. The church is in a faint distance, and the school, well, it is in shambles, so where are the children? Many are gone to the streets,

They don't know how to apply for a job. That information was deleted from the textbook. They don't know how to write a business letter. That information was deleted to. What happened to character education? No one knows because teachers are too busy trying to get the children to pass test and raise their test scores. So now, it is all about survival. Alone in the streets, many cry out, "Can you see us?"

Chapter 5

I'M HOMELESS. CAN YOU HELP ME?

(After the storm)

After the storm, the children cry

"Where is my mama, I want to die.

How do I live? How do I survive?

Is this real? Am I really alive?

In school they said,

Get your degree,

They focused on tests

And forgot about me.

My name is Johnny, the boy in back.

I was the one, whose mother's on crack.

Remember Sharon

You kept giving a pass?

She made up anything to get out of class.

Tucker Twins

She would go to the bathroom

And talk on the phone

About who she would fight

When she got them alone.

Remember the twins

Mickey and Mike?

They were the ones you really did like.

You never did see the things they would do,

Because the system had made a robot of you.

Remember Curly

You thought was so sweet,

He spat in your food

And then you would eat.

We came to school every day in a mess

But all you saw were district tests.

We had issues at home

And riding the bus.

We begged for help.

Did you see us?

I wanted to be a doctor

I knew science well

But in history you tested me

And said I had failed.

Sissy wanted to be a reporter.

She was awesome in class,

But could not pass tests

So she did not pass.

A would be politician,

Or a principal in a school

You looked passed our potential

And focused on rules.

I needed you to see me

Because home was gone.

The church had faded

I was left all alone.

The streets now have me,

Given me new chores

I'm coming for you now,

So lock your doors.

Now here is a test for you . . .

Chose the correct letter.

1. What does the author mean in the first sentence, "After the storm, the children cry, Where's my mama I want to die? " **answer:** The system failed them.

2. What can one infer about the stories of the children? **answer:** The teachers were so caught up with rules, test, and the system, that they never paid attention to the children.

3. What story does the picture tell? **answer:** Answers will vary, but the focus is the children sitting on the street as the three main institutions fade away in the background.

4. What is the author's purpose? **answer:** The author's purpose is to get the teachers and and all stakeholders in education thinking about children who have internal problems in school to see them and get then some help before it is too late.

5. Using details from the passage, explain the cause of the children's downfall. **answer:** In lines 7 & 8, the author states, "They focused on tests and forgot about me. Further down, the author states, "The system made a robot of you. In lines 26-29, the author writes that children were a mess and begged for help, but the focus was on tests and not the children. This was the downfall of the children.

6. What is the effect of the children's downfall? **answer:** They are now in the street.

7. Is the title of the poem appropriate for the message? Explain your answer. **answers will vary.**

8. What is the author's tone in this poem? **answer**: The author is warning stakeholders in education to pay close attention to children in school or it may be too late.

9. What is the mood of the poem. Use details from the passage to explain your answer. **answer**: Answers will vary.

10. What is the connotation behind the line, The streets now have me, given me new chores. I'm coming for you, so lock your doors? **Answer:** The connotation behind these lines is that the children are now being raised in a street of crime, and that the same village that was suppose to become involved in the children's lives will be destroyed by the same children they failed in the system.

Chapter 6

OLD SCHOOL VS NEW SCHOOL

The language has certainly changed through the years. It is so bad now that sometimes I find myself dummying down my own vocabulary to fit in with everyone else's so I won't feel like I am the one who is ignorant. One of my pet peeves is "This conversation is between you and I." I absolutely hate that! The conversation is never between you and I, but between you and me. Let's play a little game. This will be one you will win no doubt. Let's see if you can identify old school language vs new school language. Here is a conversation between two girls.

"Hey slut. Hy you doin girlfriend." "Um chillin Biatch. Whatchoo doin?"

"Hey Debra. How are you?" "I'm relaxing. How about yourself?"

"Wuzup Dawg?" The language spoken by children today is getting less and less intelligent. Take a look.

LOL . . . . Laugh Out loud

BRB . . . .Be right back

WTF . . . . What the fu**

OMG . . . . .Oh my God

I C U . . . .I see you.

"You is off da chain."

"You are out of your mind."

"Homeboy you trippin."

"Bruh Bruh" . . . . .Brother

"Fa wut?" . . . . . . .For what?

'Ra Ra" . . . . Talking baloney

Really doe" . . . .For real?

"An you ride chu" . . . . .You're right

"Rappin" . . . . .You don't want
to fight. You want to just talk.

"IDK" I
don't know

"TTYL" . . . . .Talk to you later

"IDC" . . . I don't care

"HMU" Hit me up"

"HRU" . . . . .How are you?

"WBU" . . . . .What about you?

"LMAO" . . . ."Laugh my ass off."

"Bumpin" . . . . .Fighting

"Wats trappin" . . . .What's up?

"UTM" . . . . .You tried me.

"ROFL . . . . .Rolling on the floor laughing

"Dueces" . . . . .Goodbye

"Bout dat life . . . . I am about that thug life .

"FYI" . . . .For your information

"LTM" . . . . Laugh to myself

"Wateves" . . . . .Whatever

"Dat" . . . . .That

"I was gonna cap to you." I was going to lie to you.

"skewl" . . . .school

"You throwed." . . . . . You don't look right

"Jit" . . . . A little child."

For ANYONE to say that it doesn't matter where a person comes from, the living conditions don't matter, or other factors surrounding the environment, when it comes to learning is sadly disillusioned. Certain individuals believe that if you are a good teacher you can save EVERYBODY. Let's look at it this way. You can have the absolute best mechanic in the world, but if you get in a car wreck, and the mechanic receives your car (product) by way of tow truck, because obviously you can't drive it, there is that one possibility that he will tell you that your car is totaled! Nothing can be done with the car after he has taken it apart and examined it all over. Is anyone going into surgery with a surgeon and tell him how to perform surgery? Is anyone telling the surgeons that their position will be tied to how many patients they lose? If a bullet hits a major artery, the patient will bleed to death. There is no saving the patient. The same thing applies to the Lawyer. Will his paycheck be tied to the number of cases he loses?

That will be HIS call wouldn't it? Yet, everyone is trying to tell a teacher how to do his or her job. Again, in any field, if a bullet hits a major artery, the patient will bleed to death.

It has been stated that people who are not in the classroom have no business telling the classroom teacher how to run his or her class. This statement is somewhat accurate. As a classroom teacher, I don't mind anyone's suggestions, but what I do mind is someone's dictatorship. I am a fan of who I believe to be the smartest man that ever lived. His name is Jesus. I am very fascinated with the parables Jesus spoke to solicit people into critical thinking.

Jesus said, . . . **"Behold, a sower went forth to sow; And when he sowed, some seeds fell by the way side, and the fowls came and devoured them up; Some fell upon stony places, where they had not much earth; and forthwith they sprung up, because they had no deepness of earth: And when the sun was up, they were scorched, and because they had no root, they withered away. And some fell among thorns; and the thorns sprung up, and choked them:**

But others fell into good ground, and brought forth fruit, some an hundredfold, some sixtyfold, some thirtyfold. Who hath ears to hear, let him hear." Now, if you are not a critical thinker, let me interpret for you. We the teachers are the sowers. Our children are our seeds.

When we pick them up and take them into a world of learning, some of our seeds may fall on stony ground, so when the sun comes up, they are burned and scorched because they had no root. If they fall among the thorns, they have fallen into the wrong crowd and will then be devoured by the thorns. Hopefully this sheds some light. There are those who will still try to tempt and challenge teachers with their same hypocrisy.

I heard a Chancellor of education say, "If you are a good teacher, it doesn't matter what the child's background is or what his living conditions are. You will save him. I did. I took 70 children who were all from an inner city school, and they had the worst scores in the school. I worked hard with them throughout the year, and at year's end, their scores rose tremendously." And what year was this? When Jesus was tempted by the Saducees and Pharisees to show them a sign from Heaven, he answered, **"When it is evening, ye say it will be fair weather: for the sky is red. And in the morning, it will be foul weather today; for the sky is red and lowering. O ye hypocrites, ye can discern the face of the sky; but can ye not discern the signs of the times?**

Therefore I ask you, "If you know your child, are you not able to discern the meaning of his cries? Are you not able to tell that something is wrong with him by merely looking upon his face?" A real teacher can do this, and a real teacher will know how to fill the prescription to making his or her child better. But note, that if the medicine is unavailable at the time, the seed may fall upon the thorns and be eaten up. Even a pharmacy may not have the medicine you need at the moment, so he will tell you to call 911. Who is 911 in the school system? These are your guidance counselors, your dropout prevention specialists, your school resource officer, your administrators, your school nurse, and other resources at the school site that can nurse your child back to help. It takes a VILLAGE, and most importantly, we must be watchful and look at our children! It is so important to stop trying to put new words on old stuff to make things sound like we are making changes and insisting that data and testing children hold the key to making education better.

What if we used terminology that will last forever like, 'DISCRETION?'. What if everyone realized that testing is not the end, but a means to an end? What if EVERYONE did his or her job? If parents did their job, and administrators did their job, then teachers can do their jobs, and then you can weed out the weak from the strong.

I heard several people speak on a popular talk show yesterday about education. The Chancellor of education stated that a teacher receives tenure after two years of teaching. Once tenure is received, a teacher cannot be fired. Unfortunately, that information was presented to the public as statement of fact, and that is not true in Florida schools. A teacher works for three years. If after three years of careful evaluations from the principal and his or her administrative staff, if the teacher's evaluation is poor, the principal can elect not to rehire the teacher in the system. As always, several people were in the audience or on stage clapping at almost anything that sounded good, but had no merit. No one appeared to be listening to the other. A young child in the audience said, "I'm smart, but I don't test well." The Billionaire said, "I'm giving money to the schools but the system I want in place is to see that teacher pay is tied to how students perform on tests. The teachers are saying, "We are now being MADE to teach to test."

The singer said," Teachers need to prepare kids to be employable and teach character education." The Chancellor said, "Let's fire them all if they don't obey." After all was said and done, it was most interesting that Charter schools were recognized at being outstanding with high graduation rates as oppose to traditional public schools. Some stated that charter schools have a lot more freedom than regular public schools. (Not a lot of dictatorship to teachers). When teachers are feeling empowered as those who are teaching in a charter school, these teachers give more of themselves because they know they are in charge of their house.

Here again, if EVERYONE does his or her part, schools would not be in critical condition. A child's first teacher is his or her mother. Education begins in the home. A teacher has no control over whether a child does his homework or not, just as a doctor has no control over whether a patient takes his prescribed medicine at home. If the parent doesn't follow the directions that the doctor prescribed for a sick child to get better, then the child will only get worse. Teachers are the mothers to all professions. However; EVERYONE IS RESPONSIBLE FOR THE GROWTH OF A CHILD! Can you see them? Open your eyes and Look!

Chapter 7

THE BOMB THAT EXPLODED

Did you know that bombs have code names? There are code names for two atomic bombs called Little Boy and Fat man. There are code names for T-N-T (explosives) However; the bomb that I was hit with is called Google. A Google bomb is an attempt to bias a search result on Google by increasing a web page's Page Rank. A successful Google bomb requires that a high number of websites (often blogs working together) link to a specific web page and the words used in the link description. The first Google bomb occurred in 1999. While the creators remain anonymous, the existence of the bomb was revealed when pjammer, a user on memepool.com, posted a question that asked what Google found to be "more evil than Satan himself." Users searching Google for the term found Microsoft's home page as the first link in the search results. The term itself was coined by Adam Mathes in 2001, when he wrote an article about how he bombed the term "talentless hack" to play a joke on a friend, graphic designer Andy Pressman.

One of the most famous Google bombs occured in 2004, when U.S. President George W.Bush was up for re-election. To experience this particular Google bomb, try searching for "miserable failure" on

Google. The first return will be a link to the biography of George W. Bush on the official White House Web site. In order for the bomb to work, a large number of Web pages had to link to the White House biography page with the authors using the exact words, "miserable failure" in their hyperlink descriptions. (definition of Google bombing . . . internet/What is a Google Bomb? Definition from Whatis.com-October 31, 2006)

In this chapter I will take you on a journey that I embarked upon in the summer of 2010 to have a voice in education that had the potential to reach millions, but the journey came to a pause for whatever reason. I am now faced with finding an alternative route in which to express my views and bring others with me who have a lot to say. Thus, *"Can You See Us,"* is born!

When you think about an explosion, you think about massive injuries or even death. You think about the loss of limbs or even war. You think about someone never being the same. In my case, I survived it all. There are no broken limbs, no massive injuries, and no death at this point. This would be another reason why unions are not around just to protect bad teachers! With the explosion that occurred around me, the union is the first organization I turned to for support and advice. Here is the story.

As an exemplary teacher in my field, I felt and still feel a strong need to go to a different level to share my experiences, and create a platform for other educators and stakeholders to voice their concerns about today's children. It is a long time coming as far as addressing educational concerns.

The opportunity presented itself when the number one talk show host of our time made an announcement that she was going to start a new chapter in her life, and start her own television network. She felt it was time to retire her television show after 25 years but wanted to give an unknown individual the opportunity to win his or her own show on the new network. I saw this as a great opportunity for my platform on educational classroom secrets and entered the competition.

In order to be in compliance with rules of the show's organization, I will only share with you my experience of what led up to the bomb that exploded on me. I need to make it clear that anything regarding my journey in the competition and what I write to completion of this book, will deal with me only. It is my hope that you will see the seriousness of what appears to be a speedy downfall of ethical principles in our society today. Thus, making it a great need to save the children before it is too late.

The competition was open to anyone from the US. You could upload a video on a show idea that you have a passion for and receive the most votes, or you could come to an open casting call audition in one of the four locations where auditions would be held in four different states. Contestants who uploaded a video wanted to be in the top five as far as votes go because the rules stated that the top five online video contestants who receive the most votes would be able to compete against other contestants selected to compete for their own show.

I entered the competition about three days after the announcement was made, and there were already approximately 50 videos on the site. I decided to work with one of my 8th grade students who is a master at computers and technology, so I asked him to work with me on this project.

Mikel obtained a camera, videotaped my presentation, and we organized a team of teachers, parents, and some former students to set up an undisclosed location to operate. I proposed a teacher reality show. I was so excited about the competition that I turned it into a summer job plus weekends. Hours of operation with a dedicated team was from 7:00A.M until6:00P.M, and after hours with family and friends taking shifts. I brought lunch for everyone. Mikel had turned me on to fast internet browsers that could increase our voting time as we clicked faster and faster sometimes working two computers at a time. Working at two colleges and four different universities and consulting with technology specialists, assisted in giving my camp a boost in our plan and resources. Our numbers were climbing faster and faster each day. For a period of time, there was one gentleman whose video remained in the number one spot. Just behind his video was a woman by the name of Marcia. Her video was receiving quite a lot of votes. It took my team a little time to restructure to climb fast. Telephone calls were made, colleagues were contacted, businesses and churches were solicited for assistance, and we began to move until we got into 3rd place. Once in 3rd place, things became fierce.

I began to gain ground when all of a sudden, the gentleman who was in 1st place dropped out of the competition, which he later posted the reason on his Facebook page. This moved Marcia into 1st place and me into 2nd place. Nevertheless, I was happy to be in a top votes spot.

Then I noticed the videos that were receiving the most views were plastered on the front page off to the side, so my team and I started asking people to view my video and drop me a comment. I began to gain ground faster and faster in viewership, votes and comments.

In the meantime overnight, I moved into 3rd place and Marcia was pushed into 2nd.

Someone had launching a Viral speed marketing campaign . Viral Speed marketing is the power to replicate and pass on information at a rapid speed. Because of my passion for education, and my competitive spirit, I felt a need to move faster and reorganize my camp. It worked. I had quickly regained the number two spot. Then the attack happened. I started gaining ground and started seeing negative posts pop up on my page. I soon found out that negative posts didn't just pop up on my page in the contest, but I was finding them EVERYWHERE! There were tons of blogs and television interviews given about the voting process. I was called ignorant and stupid in blogs. My teaching ability was questioned because of the way in which I presented my video, and negative remarks about me, Marcia, and the television talk show host started appearing all over the internet. I had been Google bombed!

The question went around the world of whether the network itself inflated votes for me.

So much publicity surrounded the competition in a matter of weeks. Allegations of cheating and rigging votes caused a whirlwind of caution, lies, deceitful plots and plans. The network released the statement. "Any allegations of impropriety will be investigated and the appropriate actions taken to keep the process unbiased." I was so stunned that I spoke with my camp and told them to slow things down hoping that the attention would go away. Against my camp's wishes, everything slowed down and pushed me back into 2nd place. There was no doubt with the resources I had, and the dedicated team, we would have come out totally ahead if it had not been for my uncomfortable feelings. Headlines made major news and I began to receive calls from reporters everywhere. I refused to talk. The key word that kept popping in my mind throughout the competition was "improprieties." I did not want anything to interfere with me going all the way in this competition.

In the meantime, the online community was having a field day with the news and sensationalism of the entire thing. Blogs were popping up everywhere. I started receiving threatening phone calls, and people even called to represent themselves as the people who were running the contest. Speculations of overzealous fans were enormous.

While working at one of my jobs, I received a phone call from someone who had stated that I had lost the contest. I was also called a "nigger" and other inappropriate names. My life along with my family members' lives were threatened if I did not drop out of the competition. Mom had received an out of area phone call from someone stating that her daughter was going to be having a 'colonoscapy'. The pizza delivery man had shown up at my parents' home several times with several boxes of pizzas that were ordered online from an unknown person. Someone had found my sister's personal information and plastered her address, phone number and any other personal information they could find on her, on the web. She too started receiving phone calls, was threatened and called "nigger." She took it a step further and filed a police report.

As time moved forward in the contest, an entire plot unfolded. One such plot was called Operation Syphyllis. The operation included allegations of botvoting, and shutting down systems. Cartoons were popping up everywhere of me in a robot body, a huge naked body with breasts hanging over my stomach, and racists remarks plastered over the body. Youtube videos began to surface, and I even made the tabloids. The worst of it all was when in a matter of three days, over 1, 269 comments were posted on a popular teacher site discrediting me as a teacher. This is when I felt that things had gone too far. How dare these grenades go off around my parents, my home, my job, and now my students!

Doc Takes The Lead

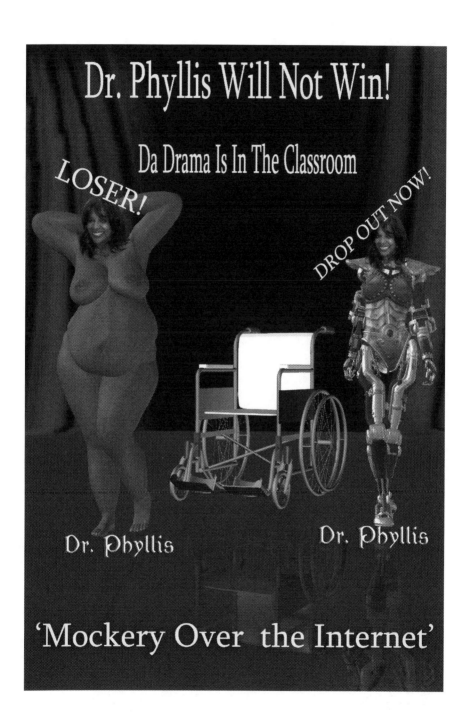

Chapter 8

RETURNING TO THE CRIME SCENE

When returning to any crime scene, the damage has to be assessed. My closest support team came to the rescue. Introducing the Bomb Squad, my family . . .

The Bomb squad

- Mr. Robert Wicks, husband
- Jeremiah Wicks, son
- Mrs. Tucker, mother
- Bishop Tucker, Father
- Dr. Philip Tucker Jr, Brother
- Dr. Pamela Jenkins, Sister-n-law
- Mentors For Ministry, Youth group

And last but certainly not least, my clone, my twin, Dr. Tucker-Johnson.

Three of the contestants came to my page quite frequently dropping me lines of support and showing love. Sometimes everyone needs a lift or boost in his or her spirit when under attack, and God has always sent protection against the enemy to surround his people.

As my team and I began to clean up the mess and clear out the debris, I contacted the captain of the team for advice.

Here is the advice that was given:

1. Pray
2. Ask and it shall be given (I didn't know what to do)
3. Seek and you shall find. (I didn't know what was next)
4. Knock and the door will open. (It seemed that I needed to close the door)
5. Watch the power! (The first will become last and the last first)
6. Believe ("I can do all things through Christ who strengthens me!)
7. Act (Faith without works is dead!)
8. Clear Your name (A good name is rather to be chosen than great riches)
9. Tame your tongue (Let the words of my mouth, and the meditation of my heart be acceptable in thy sight oh Lord)
10. Refer everyone to me for assistance! (HE IS LORD!!!!!!!!)

The Backup

Giving up is not in my nature. The desire to speak about educational issues and letting people bring their stories to the table is still prevalent for me. I suppose God prepared my platform a long time ago by giving me a husband, a son, and a beautiful family. One other such powerful miracle performed is having an identical twin, who shares my passion, has a little more experience in education than I do, and has worked 20 years as a high school teacher. She continued in her career at a center for pregnant teens, became a student intervention specialist and a dropout prevention specialist.

She began a youth ministry and transports children to and from one of our three main institutions . . . . *The Church. I suppose the message is as the Clark Sisters sing it, "It ain't over till God says it's over. You Gotta See it, before you see it, or you never will see it!" Thus,* **Double Standards in Education** *is born!*

Chapter 9

THE VISION, THE INTERVIEW, THE BEGINNING

Imagine this. My sister and I film each week in a school auditorium. We pull up in our cars coming from two different directions. The announcer is speaking. He is saying, "They have been in the school system collectively for 60 years. They have seen it all from the uppercuts to the cover-ups." When we exit our cars, we both meet in the middle and walk up the school stairs about to enter the school auditorium. The announcer continues, "They are about to present to you both sides of education. This is Double Standards In Education, Drs. Tucker-Wicks and Tucker-

Johnson." The school bell rings, and class is now in session. There are many questions. Dr.

Tucker-Wicks will go to the audience with the microphone and put twin sister Dr. Tucker-

Johnson, fondly known as Dr. TJ on the spot. Take a sneak peek . . .

Question: Dr. TJ, Why did you become a teacher?

Dr. TJ: That's quite simple. I have a true and genuine love for children.

Question: How long have you been teaching?

Dr. TJ: I am going on my 30th year.

Question: I understand you are a basketball coach as well. Are there any issues there?

Dr. TJ: This is the first year that it was announced that middle schools would be playing for championships. This puts competitive coaches with questionable ethics in the spotlight.

Question: What do you mean?

Dr. TJ: Well, the rules state that students cannot try out for the team if they do not have a 2.0 from the last nine weeks of the last school year. I was unaware that I had a student on my team who was ineligible because of this rule. I was unaware of the student at the time because I had instructed my assistant to review records. This particular student was missed. My team won against another team, and the coach from the other team had my students' records pulled to check for ineligible players. When the coach found that one of my students was found to be ineligible, he made a phone call for my team to forfeit the game.

Question: Why would this be a problem?

Dr.TJ: It would all depend on how you look at it. For example, I am also a dropout prevention specialist. This means I advocate for children. My children outplayed his team.

Technically, we won the game. In essence, the rules are basically forcing children to revisit their past and prohibit them from starting with a fresh record when they get to the next grade level. Additionally, divisiveness among coaches could create major problems, and ethical principles are now questioned.

Question: Do you not see it from the coach's perspective.

Dr. TJ: I see children.

Question: Just recently, the head of school security presented statistics on the confiscation and arrests of students who have brought firearms and or weapons to school. He showed a decline of confiscations for the past three years. How do you respond to that?

Dr. TJ: The numbers are not declining. Children are getting smarter. For example, the schools are set up for random metal detection searches. Once the police officers are on the grounds, it is announced what class they will be going into. Students merely pull out their cell phones and text their friends, *'Police On Grounds'*. Students will then begin to ask to be excused to go to the bathroom. They will hand off whatever they have in their possession that is deemed illegal. They may even go as far as to dump their contraband in a bathroom and set it on fire. Some of the students will do that and walk right off the campus.

Question: Do you think schools are too relaxed with policy?

Dr. TJ: Let me ask you this. How does one have a **modified** Zero tolerance policy? How do you have a tardy policy where a student is allowed six tardies before he/she is suspended? How many times a year do you hear a guidance counselor telling a teacher to pass children even if the children have not earned a passing grade? Have you ever heard of "administratively passing" children? For example, if a teacher doesn't pass a child at the end of the year, how does the child get promoted to the next grade level? Well, there is a double standard here. It is happening.

Question: Do you see yourself retiring from the school system soon?

Dr. TJ: I see children. I can retire as a teacher but I cannot retire from the school system. Children are a part of a school. I will keep up with them and what they are doing in school because they are a part of my ministry.

Question: If you had to do it all over again, do you see yourself becoming a teacher?

Dr. TJ: I see children. I see them in the streets, I see them in jail. I see them in school, and I see some of them in church. I started seeing many of them in my office on a one on one basis. That's when I really began not only listening, but hearing children. I heard about experiences that no child should have. I organized a group comprised of these children. Thus, Mentors For Ministry was born. I began transporting these children to church. When these children minister in church, they are in another world. All frustration comes out during ministry. These children began fondly calling me TT. TT became my nickname at my school, Dr. TT. I think I'd rather see them in school.

Question: Why did you and Dr. Tucker-Wicks come up with the title, Can You See Us?

Dr.TJ: We see children and we want others to see them too.

Question: I think the name Double Standards In Education is pretty cool. How did you come up with that one?

Dr. TJ: When I left the classroom, I started seeing the other side. I saw what was happening in the office, heard things on the walkie talkie, and witnessed things I would otherwise not witness as a classroom teacher. On the other hand, my sister is in the classroom. There can be some double standards going on here if you know what I mean.

Question: What is next for you guys?

Dr. TJ: Can you see us? Keep watching.

Chapter 10

PRINCIPALS AND OTHER ADMINISTRATORS WE HAVE LOVED
(The Dedication page)

Dr. Angela Chaniel Mr. Doug Erwin

Mr. Watts Sanderson Mr. Napoleon Wade

Mr. Vince Aguero Mrs. Sharon Tumicki

Ms. Barbara Filhart Mrs. Beverly Brown

Mr. Jimmie Ammirati Mrs. Manushka Michaud

Dr. Joyce Patterson Mr. (Pastor) Alec Richardson

Mrs. Angie Ripple

Mr. Lewis Brinson

Ms. Nadine Johnson

Dr. Joseph Brown

Mr. John Ward

Mr. Andrew Olson

Ms. Jacqueline Allen

Teaching requires many characteristics. As a teacher you feel it from all sides. You may have to face a disgruntle parent, a student who is out to get you, or a principal who doesn't like you. Either way, teaching is sure to raise stress levels.

Each year the profession becomes more and more intrusive. Various evaluation teams come into the class in groups of fives, the principal and assistant principal come in together, Peer Evaluators, Peer Mentors, Personnel from the district, personnel representing the company whose material is being used in class, parents, students who are shadowing, or it could be a person from the corporate world. If a teacher is under this kind of pressure, it will be very important to have a great leader. This section is dedicated to all of the Principals and Assistant Principals we have respected and loved because of their outstanding leadership.

One may ask the question, "What makes an outstanding leader?" That would be an effective one. Earlier in the book, an effective teacher has been defined as one who has reached the level of skill and is producing consistent effective results. An effective leader would be no different.

One who runs an effective school/organization, whereas all or most all stakeholders in the organization is producing consistent effective results, would be an indication of an effective leader. Great leaders give credibility to the statement, "Your leadership brings out the best work ethics in me." Now let's clear up the myth, "You are a born leader." Here we go again, saying things in education and buying into silliness. Great leaders are not born. If that were the case, then that would mean that a baby could lead us. Someone who is nurturing the baby who has a proven track record with leadership, would need to guide and train the baby to enhance the baby's innate leadership abilities. The nurturer cannot gain these skills without trial and error. Trial and error is called experience. Now let's pause a moment and not again get caught up into foolish sayings. For example, people say, "Experience is the best teacher." Experience is not the best teacher if one has not learned from the mistakes of the experience. This would mean that the nurturer would need to fix the mistakes and continuously improve upon them. While each mistake is being corrected, the nurturer is now increasing his or her anticipation skills, decision making skills, communication skills, and other components that come with great leadership. This would then put the nurturer on the road to producing effective results. At this point, the more experienced leader has more to offer than the less experienced one. Research shows that the most experienced people in their own field, benefit from the diversity of EXPERIENCES and viewpoints they have to offer others in the same field. Thus, the more experience one has, the better leader he or she will become. "It is not about putting down youthful vigor but about acknowledging the power of practical wisdom. Errors caused by lack of experience result in expensive waste and re-work. Experience is vital and experience delivers value. To the customer experience reassures. To the young employee experience guides. To the organization, experience is wisdom. Respecting it and nurturing it will do the organization and the nation a lot of good. Long live experience! Chella (2009).

Both my sister and I have worked for numerous principals in our collective 60 years of teaching. We cannot add all of our previous principals or administrators to this list. For us, the deep root of why we cannot, will come back to what was done with the experience they had in the field of education.

We recognize that principals and assistant principals will not make all of their teachers happy.

We also recognize that personalities can work together and personalities can clash. Administrators also have much to deal with.

We thank the above administrators for all they have done for us in making the world of teaching more pleasant.

A recollection of a rainy day after school, one of the above principals stood under a covering at the school because the rain was pouring so hard. When the bell rang, the principal approached each child who was being picked up by a parent, opened his umbrella, and personally escorted each child to his or her parent's car. It made such a lasting impression on what his children meant to him. He saw children.

Another time remembered was when a principal took a trip to Hawaii, and brought back a shirt. The principal knocked on the classroom door of a teacher the following morning and said, "I thought about you on my trip and I brought you back a shirt. That principal saw teachers.

Another administrator said, "If you ever need me, call me on the phone and just say Code Blue, and I'll be right there." That principal saw safety.

Two beautifully cushioned tall pool table chairs were donated to a teacher's classroom as the teacher was told, "You now have chairs that enhance your room and you can relax better in them after teaching your heart out to my children." That principal saw teachers and children. Others have lent their support to the black history productions that we produce every year. They provide class coverage, food for the participating children, and anything we need to be successful.

A special thank you is extended to Dr. Angela Chaniel. She is encouraging, always willing to listen, and a professional who is a great communicator. If the leader does his or her job correctly, the organization would run smoothly. Thanks guys!

Chapter 11

Tribute to an Educator
The Ms. Maebell McDaniel Story
April 1935-June 2000
Story told by Phyllis

Ever since I was a little girl I heard my mother say her biggest dream when she was a little girl was to grow up and live in the projects. I never really questioned her words until I got a little older to understand that living in the projects is seen as derogatory. As I look on it now, it is clear to me that the projects back in my mother's time period was special. There was something called pride back in her time. People who lived in the projects took care of their apartments. They kept their places clean as well as the neighborhood. Today however, the projects is known as the hood. It is infested with crime in some places, and in some instances, living conditions are bad.

I clearly remember the day that my eyes were opened when she made that statement. I was sitting down in the living room in our family's beautiful three bedroom two bath home. Mom and I were having a conversation. Again she repeated as she had so often said,

"My biggest dream when I was a little girl was to move into the projects." I questioned her for the first time.

"What do you mean? Why do you say that? That's stupid," I said. Mom responded by saying that living in the projects was her biggest dream because she came from the alley. Well everyone knows when you think of an alley, you think of crawling creatures of any species, garbage, unclean waste, bums, and anything else connected to the word "disgusting". I didn't believe her at first. It wasn't until she produced a picture of an old shack of a house that was located in the middle of an alley. The house was so small that when you walked in the front door, you exited the back.

There were seven members who lived in the house. There were my grandparents, Mom, and her four other siblings. The family was very poor. My grandmother worked in people's homes and scrubbed toilets and cleaned their houses. My grandfather was basically a minister for a church. Back then, it was hard for African Americans. My grandparents did whatever they had to so that the family could eat.

When my aunt Maebell was born, she became my mom's favorite sibling as Maebell was the baby of the family. When Maebell turned three years old, she began to get sick and run high fevers. She started complaining a lot about her legs hurting. The family could not afford a doctor so family members took turns staying up with Maebell late at night until she would go to sleep. My mother stayed up the most. She would pack cold cloths on Maebell's forehead as Maebell would get really hot.

As Maebell grew up, the pains were increasing. The pain got so bad that it became hard for her to stand so she began to crawl. Maebell crawled and barely walked until she was nine years old. My mother wanted Maebell to go to school when she became of age, so my mother would lift Maebell during her first few years of her life and carry her to school piggy back style. When Maebell reached age seven, a doctor in the neighborhood heard about her, and agreed to see her for free. When the doctor diagnosed her, he found she had contacted Polio. Polio is a crippling disease for which there was no real cure back then. However, the doctor recommended that my grandmother take Maebell to the All Children's Hospital in St. Petersburg Florida to use the machines for crippled people. This was great therapy. He strongly felt that using the machines would help her regain strength in her legs and she could possibly walk again. How? How were they going to get to St. Pete? There was no money, so the family continued to nurse Maebell at night while she screamed in excruciating pain.

Finally, my grandmother was able to save up enough money to take Maebell to St. Petersburg, Florida. Unfortunately, upon arrival at the hospital, A white gentlemen greeted my grandmother at the door and told her that blacks were not allowed to use the machines there. This took a real toll on my mother. She loved her baby sister, and to be told that her sister may never be able to walk again if she did not have access to machines that were clearly usable because of skin color, devastated her.

When my grandmother took Maebell back to the doctor, the doctor explained that one of Maebell's legs would outgrow the other. She would need two pairs of shoes as Maebell would have one big foot and one little foot. She also told my grandmother that something else on Maebell would grow very big on her body and that she would have a lot of weight to carry. His recommendation was to get Maebell some crutches to support her weight.

During this time period, my mom would continue to carry Maebell to school until my grandmother was able to purchase crutches. Maebell's breast began to grow at a rapid speed. Her breast grew so large that when she grew older and started getting her annual checkups, the doctor would tell her to throw her right breast over her shoulder to check her belly, and she would repeat the same motions with the left breast.

My mother began to have thoughts in her head about how she could heal Maebell. At one point she started thinking that there was some kind of chemical in dirt that could stimulate the muscles in Maebell's legs. As a result of her thinking, she would dig a deep hole in a close neighbor's home and bury her sister from the waist down in the dirt everyday after school. When my mother began to figure out that her remedy was not working, she started crying consistently.

One day my grandmother approached my mother and asked her why she was crying. My mother told my grandmother that she no longer wanted to live in the alley. She told her mother that she wanted out. My grandmother's response was, "If you want to get out of the alley then you have to get your education. Your education can take you out of the alley." From that day forward, my mother would continue to study and motivate my aunt to do well in school and get her education.

Both Ms. Maretha McDaniel and Ms. Maebell McDaniel went to college after high school.

Each would pursue education to become teachers in Hillsborough County. It took my aunt several years to get a job in the county because there was no faith in the system that a crippled woman could do well as a teacher. It didn't matter that my aunt was a strong and intelligent woman. She never made any excuses about her handicap and certainly didn't use it to obtain sympathy from anyone. I could imagine her saying," I was a woman. I was black. I was cripple, but I am a survivor. All were considered handicaps. Life is too short. I move forward." Nevertheless, she was told by several principals that they would not hire her because they didn't think she could handle the students. Seems that everybody thought my aunt was handicapped except my aunt.

My mother and aunt began to write legislators, and other politicians for assistance. My mother was insistent about my aunt having the same opportunity she had in becoming a teacher.

She didn't want to see her sister struggle to get a job. Mom was so persistent that she approached the principal at her school about hiring my aunt. Unfortunately, family members could not work at the same school back then, so my mother quit her job so that my aunt could work. Finally, Ms. Maebell McDaniel became a teacher! She had many interesting stories in this field called education.

Once, a student took her crutches and through them on the top of the roof at the school. Another time she was sucking on a toothpick while sitting at her desk. Her desk drawer was open and a student made her mad. She was so upset that she quickly closed her desk drawer and her breast got caught in the drawer. She even took students on fieldtrips. For example, when I was little, my aunt wanted to take her students on their first train ride. She organized everything, and had students pack their lunches. She secured chaperones, and made it happen. She invited me and my sister, and we had the time of our lives.

Ms. Maebell McDaniel valued education and always thirsted for more knowledge. She went back to school to obtain her Master's degree in Business Administration. She bought her own home down the street from my mother who had gotten married and had three children. My aunt had her home custom designed to fit her needs as well as the Mercedes and Buick she drove. She travelled all over the world before she passed in June 2000. She was a faithful member of Beulah Baptist church under the leadership of the legendary Rev.

Leon A. Lowry, who was a prominent local Civil rights leader that once taught Dr. Martin Luther King Jr., and led the desegregation of public facilities.

Ms. McDaniel never married, but like me, my sister, and my mother, we became the mothers to thousands of children. She spoke to children about overcoming challenges. For African Americans, there were many. I remember my mother telling me that there used to be the Black water fountains, and White water fountains. When my aunt became 10, her boldness grew as she reflected upon the slight chance to walk again when she was younger, but denied an opportunity to use machines because she was black. This made her daring.

There were many times my grandmother had to go to the courthouse for various reasons. She would take my mother and Maebell with her. In the lobby, the signs were boldly written above two separate water fountains. One sign would read "Colored", and the other would read "Whites".

According to the autobiography of Miss Jane Pittman, it took Jane some odd years to boldly walk up to a White water fountain to drink. For 10yr old Maebell, she would purposely get away from my mother in the courthouse, leaving my mother calling out for her. "Where are you?," she called. Maebell would shout as loud as she could, "I'm drinking white water!" She would purposely wait until a white person was around and hobble up to the "Whites Only" water fountain on crutches and drink. "No one bothered her", said my mother as a tear streamed down her beautiful brown face while telling me Maebell's story. I guess they were too scared to bother a black girl on crutches in a courthouse."

I consider Ms. Maebell McDaniel an unsung hero in education along with many others my sister and I have been blessed to have been touched by. There were: Mrs. Maretha Tucker, Mr. Herbert Kinsey, Ms. Marion Speight, Ms. Lula Daye, Ms. Linda Fernandez, Mrs. Sarah Zewadski, Ms. Patricia Cooper, Mrs. Carolyn Everett, Mrs. Susan Davis, Mrs. Marie Wimberly, Dr. Brian Adams, Mrs. Hattie Crawford, Mrs. Betty Simmons, Mrs. Betty Kinsey, Mrs. Delois Sheppard, Mr. Ricky Tyson, Mr. Heaton, Verlynda Bell, and Mrs. Alyndria Miller, and Mrs. Kietta Mayweather-Gamble.

These too are our veterans fighting everyday for our country. They too are soldiers going to war facing "New school," to include the rapes, murders, assaults, bombs, and other heinous crimes. They too have to go through the boot camp of professional development, evaluations, disgruntle parents or students, record keeping, and ultimately saving lives. They have to keep their troops out of the enemy's line of fire called ignorance. They too have to pledge. However, they pledge their allegiance to children. The difference is . . . Teachers arm themselves with paper, pens, books and knowledge. They provide the tools necessary for all other occupations including the soldier who goes to war. Therefore, for the purpose of this book, Drs. Tucker-Wicks and Johnson salute our veterans . . . . . . Veteran teachers that is.

Afterword

The purpose of this book is to serve as an eye opener for educators and non educators. We all need to open our eyes and see children. Thus, we need to see our future. To not pay attention to our children is like not paying attention to ourselves. Isn't it amazing how a child is born with no past, but holds the future in his hands, and some adults who have a past can't see a future?

People will often say, "No one can predict the future." Of course you can. If one looks back in the past, one can certainly predict the future. For example, if yesterday I stuck my hand in a fire and received 3rd degree burns, then certainly I can predict that if I do the same in the future, the consequences may be the same. The weather man can predict the weather because of what the weather has done in the past. He knows how to protect himself because of past experiences.

Oops. I said the word again . . . . Experiences.

John Adams wrote a letter to Thomas Jefferson on April 19, 1817. He wrote, "Without religion, this world would be something not fit to be mentioned in polite company, I mean Hell." In a letter written to Abigal on the day the Declaration was approved by congress,

Adams wrote, "July 4th ought to be commemorated as the day of deliverance by solemn acts of devotion to God Almighty. The general principles upon which the fathers achieved independence were the general principles of Christianity . . . I will avow that I believed and now believed that those general principles of Christianity are as eternal and immutable as the existence and attributes of God." It worked! What have we learned from that? Was it to take prayer out of schools? In our past experiences, the children were being raised by the village. It worked! What have we learned from that? Was it to dissolve the village? In our past experiences, spanking children was an acceptable form of discipline. It worked! What have we learned from that? Was it to provide an abuse hotline? In our past experiences, pants were worn about the waist, makeup was lessened, and shorts were a little longer. It worked! What have we learned from that? Was it to have children look like thugs and women for hire? In our past experiences, parents told children where their place was. It worked! Was it to let children tell their parents where their place is, now known as "My space?" What have we learned from that? The point here is clear. If we want to see a bright future, we must learn from past experiences.

Let's see what kept us safe, society productive, and the environment clean. We must stop trying to fix what was never broken just to justify poor decision making, inexperience, prestige seeking, self interest bombs waiting to explode that will ultimately wipe us all out. See the children. Shape them. Mold them. Stop stealing from them. Stop stealing their education, their money and their self-esteem. Let's give back to them what our forefathers gave to us . . . In our forefathers' understanding, in order to have a strong society; you must have strong education, but in order to have strong education, you must build that education upon Christian principles and the Word of God. Benjamin Rush once said, "the only foundation for a useful education in a republic, is to believe in religion (Christianity). Without this, there could be no virtue, and without virtue, there could be no liberty. And liberty is the only object and life of all republican governments. Without religion, I believe that learning does real mischief to the morals and principles of mankind." We must see the children and bring some past back. It is vital to our survival! Then and only then can we be assured that **WE** are not creating weapons of Mass destruction!

0030354 XX DS

Poetrygram

We are awarding you
HONORABLE MENTION

You will be pleased to know as of this contest,
you have won 2 Award of Merit Certificates!

FEBURARY 20, 1987

PHYLLIS TUCKER
1718 ARCH ST
TAMPA FL 33607

Thank you for entering our GREAT BONUS Poetry Contest. Our Poetry Editor &
Judge Eddie-Lou Cole has awarded your fine poem TO BE A TEACHER an
HONORABLE MENTION. I know you'll want to frame and display your Award of
Merit Certificate with pride. We are quite proud of you here at World of
Poetry. Enclosed herewith is a complete winners list. Keep up the good
work!

JOSEPH MELLON, Contest Director

World of Poetry • 2431 Stockton Boulevard • Sacramento, California 95817 • Telephone (916) 731-8463

Tear along perforation

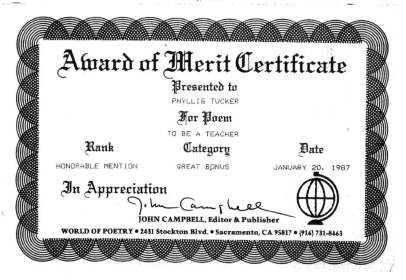

Award of Merit Certificate

Presented to
PHYLLIS TUCKER

For Poem
TO BE A TEACHER

Rank	Category	Date
HONORABLE MENTION	GREAT BONUS	JANUARY 20, 1987

In Appreciation

JOHN CAMPBELL, Editor & Publisher

WORLD OF POETRY • 2431 Stockton Blvd. • Sacramento, CA 95817 • (916) 731-8463

0030354

| SILVER POET AWARD FOR 1986 | **Poetrygram**® |

December 16, 1986

PHYLLIS TUCKER
1718 ARCH ST
TAMPA FL 33607

It is a pleasure to send you your Silver Poet Award for 1986.
Please frame and display it with pride. All of us at World of
Poetry are very proud of you. Happily, we have enclosed
information on our Great Bonus Poetry Contest. As a Silver
Poet you are cordially invited to enter. Bless you!
                    --EDDIE-LOU COLE, Poetry Editor

𝔚𝔬𝔯𝔩𝔡 𝔒𝔣 𝔭𝔬𝔢𝔱𝔯𝔶 2431 Stockton Blvd. • Sacramento, California 95817 • Telephone (916) 731-8463

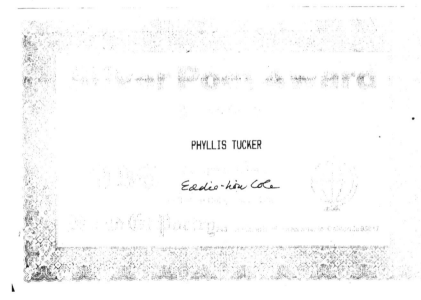

PHYLLIS TUCKER

Eddie-Lou Cole

Congratulations!
World of Poetry's Board of Directors
has elected to honor you with our
GOLDEN POET AWARD FOR 1987

Poetrygram

PHYLLIS TUCKER
1718 ARCH ST
TAMPA FL 33607

May 9, 1987

Dear Poet:

I am so excited to tell you the good news!

World of Poetry's Board of Directors has voted unanimously to honor you with our Golden Poet Award for 1987, in recognition of your remarkable poem TO BE A TEACHER which you recently entered in our GREAT BONUS POETRY CONTEST. New poets ask: What is the Golden Poet Award? Like I say to the media: The Golden Poet Award is to poets what the Academy Award is to actors. It is the highest honor World of Poetry is able to bestow on a poet.

The presentation will take place at our Third Annual Poetry Convention, on Tuesday afternoon, August 11, at one o'clock, at the Las Vegas Hilton, in Las Vegas, Nevada. Then, during our Golden Banquet at 7:30 pm, after John Campbell has presented a special program in your honor, you will participate in our fabulous Golden Parade, complemented by the World of Poetry Orchestra. The evening promises to be so spectacular, World Television will be there to record the event.

Many poets are coming to our convention alone; many with guests. Either way, we can accomodate you. I have enclosed a copy of our May-June newsletter which outlines every detail of our convention. In addition, it will show you how to register, how to make hotel and airline reservations--all at special convention discounts.

There will be so many poets and celebrities to meet, like Milton Berle. There will be so many wonderful things to do, so many things to experience and learn. As a Golden Poet, you'll want to pick one of your best poems to enter in our Convention Poetry Contest. I am almost 80-years young and it would do my heart good to see you win one of our ten $1,000 First Prizes, or indeed our $15,000 Grand Prize, and be crowned our Poet Laureate for 1987. It could happen. Just ask Jeanne Losey, who won last year!

If I can be of further help, please let me hear from you.

In Love and Admiration,

Eddie-Lou Cole
EDDIE-LOU COLE, Poetry Editor

P.S. As a poet I'll bet you are always doing nice things for others. It is time to do something nice for yourself. See you in Las Vegas!

World Of Poetry 2431 Stockton Blvd. • Sacramento, California 95817 • Telephone (916) 731-8463

References

Ellis, Dave (2009). Becoming A Master Student. Boston New York: Houghton Mifflin Company.

Plaguer, PJ. (1983). Computer Language Retrieved March 4, 2010 from internet

New King James Version Bible

encyclopedia2.thefreedictionary.com/Google+bomb

About the Authors

Drs. Phyllis and Philetha Tucker have been teaching in Hillsborough County Schools collectively for 60 years. They both have their BA degrees in English Education and Master degrees in Educational Leadership. Both ladies have their Doctorate degrees in Education and are presented as Double Standards in Education on various speaking platforms. The former Buccaneer cheerleaders share much of the same awards to include Who's Who among great teachers, former talk show hosts, Miss Black Florida, Miss Black America, Black Diamond award winner(s), Educator(s) of the year on the college circuit, and Unsung heroes at the annual Dr. Martin Luther King Jr. ceremony.

Dr. Phyllis is an adjunct professor at Nova Southeastern University, Southwest Florida College, Hillsborough Community College, and an online finalist for the Oprah Winfrey network to have her own television talk show. Both ladies are adjunct professors at University Of Phoenix.